Ursula Brecht

Precious Dolls

A Treasury of Bisque Dolls

Ursula Brecht

Precious Dolls

A Treasury of Bisque Dolls

HPBooks®

Credits

Gertrud Kolmar: *The Doll*, from Gertrud Kolmar, Das Lyrische Werk. Kösel-Verlag, Munich, 1960. With the kind permission of Kösel-Verlag, Munich.

Ursula Wölfel: *The Toy Store*, from Lesewerk Wunder Welt 1968, Band II. Pädag. Verlag Schwann, Düsseldorf. With the kind permission of Ursula Wölfel.

Executive Editor: Rick Bailey
Editorial Director: Randy Summerlin
Editor: Jacqueline Sharkey
Art Director: Don Burton
Book Design: Leslie Sinclair
Typography: Cindy Coatsworth, Michelle Claridge
Translation: Ruth A. Lewis and John S. Lewis
Technical Consultant: Mildred Seeley

HPBooks®

P.O. Box 5367
Tucson, AZ 85703
(602) 888-2150
ISBN: 0-89586-330-8
Library of Congress Catalog Card Number: 84-80435
© 1984 Fisher Publishing, Inc.
Printed in U.S.A.

Originally published in Germany as *Kostbare Puppen*
© 1980 by Kunstverlag Weingarten GmbH, Weingarten

Dedication

This book is dedicated to my mother and family, who have been so patient and understanding regarding my doll collecting and photography.

I especially want to thank Alfred Barsotti for his advice and support. I also want to thank Folkert Mindermann, whose encouragement gave me the incentive to create this book. I'm grateful to my friends in England who allowed me to photograph their interesting and beautiful collections, and to everyone who contributed to this book's success.

Editor's Note to English Edition

Recent research has uncovered new information regarding the French doll-making firm, *Gaultier*. The founder, François Gaultier, originally spelled his last name *Gauthier*. He changed the spelling in 1875. This book uses the name François Gaultier.

Some books refer to *Ferdinand* or *Fernand* Gaultier, but no such doll maker existed. Confusion about Gaultier's first name resulted from errors made by researchers prior to the mid-1960s.

Definitive research that has cleared the name confusion on the Gaultier firm was done by Florence Poisson, conservator of the Musée Roybet-Fould in Courbevoie, France. The results of her work were published in 1982 in Bulletin No. 7 of the Centre d'Étude et de Recherche sur les Poupées, in Courbevoie.

Photo Captions

Most caption titles in this book list only one maker of a doll, even though the head may have been made by one firm and the body by another. Complete information about the makers of a doll was not available in most cases.

Dates in captions are approximate. They are the years when the types of dolls shown in the photographs were first made.

Table of Contents

Bisque, French, Gaultier, marked _F.10 G._
Premiere Gaultier is a rare doll made by François Gaultier, Paris, about 1878. The doll has finely painted swivel head with closed mouth and stationary, dark, blue-gray paperweight eyes. She has ball-jointed, wood-and-composition body.

How My Doll Collection Began

During my childhood, before World War II, I was allowed to rummage through the attic in our house. I was fascinated by all the old boxes and trunks. They held so many mysteries that going through them was always an adventure.

One day, I found a trunk filled with silk-and-lace dresses from my grandmother's childhood. As I took out the dresses I found an old, jointed doll lying among them. She had a delicate, finely molded porcelain head, expressive glass eyes and a disheveled, curly wig.

Her trousseau was in a small wicker hamper. It was filled with beautiful, hand-sewn dresses, lacy shirts, frilly stockings and ankle-length boots. They were items that a mother would have used 50 years earlier to dress up her daughter.

The doll was a dream from a bygone era, and she filled me with wonder. She became the center of my fantasies. I spent hours inventing stories about her.

Sadly, these games ended with the war. Our house was destroyed during a bombing raid. Along with everything else, I lost the doll. But I never lost hope of finding another like her.

When the war was over, my family and I had a difficult time. Years passed, and I didn't have an opportunity to look for a doll. Then, shortly after my wedding day, my husband and I visited a flea market in Paris. As I looked through a pile of antiques, I saw her. She had threadbare, dusty clothes, a moth-eaten wig and a lovely porcelain face.

Immediately the old fascination returned. I wanted more than anything to buy that doll and take her home. But I could not. There were other, more important things to buy.

In the ensuing years, I was busy caring for our children and the house. I had no chance to resume my search for a doll. But the desire to find one remained strong.

Then one day about 15 years ago, as I walked through Cologne, I passed an antique shop. I glanced casually in the window and there they were. More than 20 dolls of different sizes were standing and sitting in the display case. Some were leather, others had wood joints. But they all had porcelain faces with large, clear eyes that spoke of a world far removed from the gray, humdrum city.

I stared at the window, then entered the shop. I picked up the dolls one by one. I moved their arms and legs, and rotated their heads. Once again I fell under the spell cast by my playmate so many years before. I felt like a child standing in front of a Christmas tree.

One doll appealed to me more than the others. She was small, dainty and dressed in a light-blue, original frock. She had a sensitive face with a lovely expression. She became the first doll in my collection.

The day after I brought her home, I began to take pictures of her. I posed her at the fireside, in the garden, among the autumn leaves. Photographing her became a fascinating, relaxing pastime.

Bisque, French, Gaultier, marked _F.6 G._ in a scroll. Made about 1885, this doll has typical Gaultier face, with closed mouth and fixed, brown paperweight eyes.

Before long, I returned to the antique shop and bought another doll. I knew nothing at this time about differences among dolls. I didn't even know about markings on the backs of their heads and necks, indicating who made them and what series they were part of.

I learned quickly. I began examining dolls very closely, as an expert collector would. I lifted their hair to examine their markings. I removed their clothing to check the condition of their bodies. But I looked most carefully at their faces. I kept searching for the expression of my childhood doll, an expression I had kept in my heart all those years.

And I began to find it. In small antique shops, flea markets and auction houses, I located dolls that looked like mine, dolls that had watched children growing up in the nurseries of my grandmother's time.

Collecting became an all-consuming interest. I searched relentlessly for dolls I wanted, then spent hours bargaining for them. After bringing the dolls home, I spent weeks mending, rewiring and restoring them. When these tasks were completed, I photographed my acquisitions.

I learned a great deal in those early days about the highs and lows of collecting. I unwittingly paid exorbitant prices when I started because I didn't know what made one doll worth more than another. Some dealers tried to sell me forgeries. Others tried to pass restored dolls as originals.

But gradually I learned. I found books that provided basic guidelines for buying dolls and experienced collectors who were willing to share their knowledge with me. These collectors taught me that dolls with closed mouths are the oldest and rarest. They explained that I should look for dolls with faces of very light bisque, because that type of porcelain is the finest.

I began studying German and French dolls. I compared the characteristics of dolls made by German firms such as Armand Marseille, Simon & Halbig, and Kämmer & Reinhardt. I learned the techniques used by French doll makers such as Jumeau, Gaultier, Gesland and Steiner.

I will never forget the moment I held my first Jumeau. She had a closed mouth and beautiful original clothing. She was my most expensive possession, but her charm and lovely expression captivated me.

This is why my enthusiasm for collecting has never waned. Searching and acquiring each doll is a unique, exciting experience. I feel such childlike joy when I find a new doll and hold her in my arms for the first time, marveling at her beauty.

Collecting is a passion that exists independently of what is being collected. People can lose themselves in the objects they covet, whether those be paintings or postcards, stamps or sculpture.

All collectors lead existences centered around the search for particular pieces. As they begin looking for something they want, they are tormented with uncertainty. Will they be able to find this special item? If they find it, will they be able to buy it? As the search continues they become obstinate, willing to put up with any inconvenience to acquire the object of their dreams. They become experts at accomplishing the impossible.

Finally, they experience the exhilaration of holding that rare item for the first time, or the grief of discovering they cannot possess it after all. They are intensely happy or deeply depressed.

But regardless of the outcome of a particular search, collectors are basically contented people. They are full of fantasies and hope. They are never bored. Their lives are full of surprises. Each day is different.

Collectors don't care whether the object has monetary value or value only in their hearts. Their love of collecting has its own rewards. It provides memories linked with their childhoods. It provides objects that bring renewed happiness each time they are seen or touched.

This is certainly what collecting has meant to me. I would spend weeks or months searching for a doll I wanted, and would feel genuinely fulfilled when I finally brought her home.

I must confess that my activities created some problems. In the beginning, my family was less than understanding as I populated our living room with dolls that had lived in other people's homes decades earlier.

They were more upset when I brought in little beds, tables, stools and wagons, all in dismal condition. I converted part of the house into a workshop and spent days reconstructing dolls, and stripping and painting tiny pieces of furniture.

My husband and children were dismayed by this at first. But eventually they began smiling indulgently. Finally they accepted my activities completely. I am very grateful for their forbearance.

As my collection grew larger, I continued to learn, as most collectors do. My viewpoint changed. I paid more attention to details, and my standards became more exacting. I didn't repeat the blunders I had made in the beginning.

Over the years, I clarified my ideas concerning what I wanted my collection to be. One charming characteristic of doll collectors is the distinctive way each develops a collection. Some work like scholars. They research the origins and development of dolls. Their acquisitions provide a museumlike view of doll-making's history.

Some collectors are interested only in dolls made of one material, such as porcelain, wax or wood. Others collect one type of doll, such as Character Dolls or Fashion-Type Dolls.

The uniqueness of dolls provides collecting with its liveliness and sense of originality.

As I continued acquiring dolls, I found myself increasingly drawn to those with beautiful faces. I enjoyed the German dolls, but the French dolls were my favorites. Their faces, with huge paperweight eyes and finely drawn features, were less childlike. They had serious,

contemplative expressions and a noble quality that fascinated me.

After I clarified my goals, I began organizing my collection. I separated the dolls I had chosen in the beginning for emotional reasons from those I had selected after gaining experience. I sold or traded those early dolls for newer, more interesting pieces. It made me sad, but I had to do it to keep my collection from getting out of control.

By this time my children had grown, so I could search for dolls in more distant places. In the early years, I confined myself to Cologne and Düsseldorf, but now I traveled throughout Europe.

I had many new experiences as I met international dealers. I saw splendid collections and photographed some of them. I browsed through fairs in England and helped run a display at an auction in Switzerland.

Eventually, I set up my own booth at a collectors' exchange, where I sold only one doll. Despite this less-than-overwhelming commercial success, I learned a great deal. I also met some interesting doll fanciers, including some lovable idealists. We discussed the joy and pain of collecting and the concerns and problems facing buyers and sellers. It was an unforgettable time, and the information I acquired and the people I encountered more than compensated for the lack of profit.

On one of my trips to London, I discovered the antique markets, an El Dorado for collectors.

They were full of lovely accessories that add beauty and value to any collection. I also met a group of active collectors and dealers who frequently had rare pieces to sell.

Collecting has enriched my life. The collection itself is a constant source of happiness that lives with me. Through photographs, the collection changes constantly. It inspires my imagination and creates a world in which I can lose myself in childhood fantasies.

Why I Photographed My Collection

Precious Dolls is a picture book to be perused and enjoyed at leisure. It is not a specialty book abounding in details, although numerous details here are worthy of discussion. Doll collecting continually opens new avenues for people to explore. Many specialty publications provide important information for collectors, and I have used them since I began acquiring dolls.

But the purpose of this book is different. I am not trying to convey information about these dolls, but to describe them in an artistic way.

When I began working on this photographic anthology, I wanted to produce luminous portraits of my acquisitions. Each doll is unique, with a distinctive appearance and expression. Some look thoughtful or dreamy. Others seem faintly amused or astonished by what they see. Many look cool and aloof, almost arrogant.

The driving force behind my photography was the desire to capture these expressions. I have tried to do this by photographing the dolls in different ways. Some are pictured alone, others in groups. Some are in a garden, others by a Christmas tree.

I have photographed some dolls more than once to show the different sides of their characters. I have always been impressed by the way these dolls change expression when their heads are moved slightly. They take on entirely different personalities.

I started taking pictures of my collection the day after I bought my first doll. Each new doll inspired me to try to capture her spirit in a photograph. I have attempted to paint a portrait of each doll with my camera.

I discovered that one effective way to do this was to photograph the dolls with flowers in the background. At first I simply did this intuitively. I would see blossoms outside in the soft spring light or a bouquet on a table, and I would realize they provided the perfect setting for particular dolls. The play of colors against the dolls' pale complexions seemed a perfect expression of their incandescent beauty.

Naturally, I served an apprenticeship in photography. I made many mistakes in the beginning. I didn't realize that a porcelain face was too light to be photographed in the midday sun. Instead of showing a doll's expressive, finely molded features, my early pictures showed only a flat, white, round disk. I eventually learned I had to put dolls in shadowed areas to get the correct modeling of the face.

I also found I had to calculate my film exposures carefully when photographing dolls in white dresses. These charming old dresses reflected a great deal of light and made the entire picture look overexposed.

For years I took all my pictures outdoors during the day. I liked working with natural light and shadow. They gave my pictures a softer quality and made contours less sharp.

For the past several years, I have often set up a lamp to one side of the dolls in the pictures. This additional light gives eyes and hair more luster,

Bisque, French, Bru, marked Bru Jne 14. Voice box that says "Mama" is feature of doll by Leon Casimir Bru, Paris. Voice mechanism was inserted in the middle of her jointed, composition body, which is held together by a leather band. Cord on one side of body controls voice box. When cord is pulled, doll says "Mama." Made about 1879, doll has beautifully modeled swivel head. With her closed mouth and fixed, blue-gray paperweight eyes, she is especially expressive.

and provides pleasing shadows in the folds of costumes.

Despite my progress, I am always impressed and filled with self-doubt when I see other photographers' work. Their pictures seem so perfect. The composition is precise, and the dolls have often been photographed in historic environments.

I believe that photography, like collecting, reflects the attitudes and feelings of the individual. Both photographers and collectors use their work to convey their ideas. For example, my pictures are less structured than most photographers'. The ideas for them occur spontaneously. I will look at a doll and suddenly get an inspiration about how to photograph her.

When I began taking pictures, I never thought they would be used for anything but providing enjoyment for me and information for other collectors. After all, I was inexperienced photographically. I was guided much more by my eye than by technology.

During those early years, I used print film. I filled numerous albums with beautiful pictures. None are in this book, however. Prints don't reproduce well, so my first photographic efforts can only be seen in my albums. I finally made the switch to slides, which are better suited to publishing, when my husband's firm asked me to produce a doll calendar.

The production of this book has been a wonderful adventure for me, especially in light of my slow, painstaking education in photography. I believe my pictures convey some of the pleasure this undertaking has given me. Everyone likes to experience and share beautiful things. My lovely dolls have been a source of great joy, and I have tried to use my camera to help others share that joy.

German Dolls

Bisque, German, Simon & Halbig, marked *S.H. 1249 DEP. Germany 12 Santa.* Simon & Halbig, Gräfenhain, Germany, gave *Santa,* on page 21, a swivel head with glass, brown sleep eyes. Ball-jointed body is composition and wood.

Bisque, German, Simon & Halbig, marked *S H 1010-14 DEP.* This doll has a beautiful shoulder head with glass, blue sleep eyes. Body is leather, with molded bisque forearms and hands.

The German dolls described here are all in good—although not always original—condition. Many have newer wigs or repaired hands or other limbs. The clothing is mostly from a later date. This does not diminish the charm of these dolls, however. It shows that they were often played with. The scarcer and more expensive dolls could be handled by children only on Sundays or holidays, and then only under supervision. This is one reason why these expensive, well-preserved dolls can still be found in good condition.

Bisque, German, head by Simon & Halbig, body by Kämmer & Reinhardt, marked *Simon & Halbig K(star)R.*
Doll has molded eyebrows, real eyelashes, and glass, blue sleep eyes. Kämmer & Reinhardt, Waltershausen, Germany, made ball-jointed body of wood and composition.

Bisque, marked 3.
Closed mouth, called a *pouty mouth,* gives this unsigned doll a willful expression. She has a small, swivel head with glass, blue sleep eyes. Composition body is jointed.

Bisque, possibly German, marked S 3.
Doll has an open mouth and fixed, blue eyes. Wood-and-composition body is jointed.

Bisque, German, Schmidt, marked *BSW 13*.
Bruno Schmidt, Waltershausen, Germany, made this doll. She has a jointed, composition body, and swivel head with open mouth. Blue sleep eyes are glass.

Bisque, German, heads by Simon & Halbig, bodies by Kämmer & Reinhardt.
Mein Liebling, opposite page, doll in center, is described in caption at lower left. Character Doll on right is marked *K(star)R Simon & Halbig 116/A 32.* Doll has swivel head with merry, glass, blue sleep eyes and open-closed mouth with molded tongue. Body is composition, with movable but unjointed arms and legs. Character Doll on left is marked *K(star)R Simon & Halbig 115/A 34.* She has swivel head with glass, brown eyes and closed, pouty mouth. Jointed body is composition.

Bisque, German, head by Simon & Halbig, body by Kämmer & Reinhardt, marked *K(star)R Simon & Halbig 117 58*.
Mein Liebling (My Darling) has swivel head with glass, blue sleep eyes and closed mouth. Name relates to her childlike expression.

Bisque, German, head by Simon & Halbig, body by Kämmer & Reinhardt, marked **K (star) R Simon & Halbig 116/A 32.** Detail of doll described on page 26.

Bisque, German, head by Simon & Halbig, body by Kämmer & Reinhardt, marked **S & H K (star) R 34.** Doll has swivel head and glass, blue sleep eyes. Jointed body is composition. Shown larger on page 122.

Bisque, German, Kämmer & Reinhardt.
Boy Character Doll is marked *109* and girl Character Doll is marked *114.* Both have beautiful swivel heads with expressive faces. Bodies are composition. Both are from Jackie Jacobs Collection, London.

**Bisque, German, marked
289 DEP.**
This doll has a beautifully
painted swivel head with
fixed, glass, brown eyes
and open mouth. Her
composition-and-wood
body is ball-jointed.

**Bisque, possibly German,
marked 167-2 on the
shoulder plate.**
Elegant bisque forearms
and hands are among the
loveliest characteristics
of the doll on opposite
page. She has a closed
mouth and fixed, glass,
bright-blue eyes. Body is
fine leather, with elegant
bisque forearms and
hands.

**Bisque, German, marked
L.**
A very fair shoulder head,
open mouth and glass,
blue sleep eyes make this
doll, right, especially
attractive. Body is fine
kid. Forearms and hands
are carefully molded
bisque.

**Bisque, German, Schmidt,
marked Made in Germany
B S W 12 on the heart.**
The doll above has a
swivel head with lashed,
glass, brown flirty eyes.
Her jointed body is
composition.

Sleep, My Little Doll

(Original German title: *Schlafe, mein Püppelein*)

And now, little doll,
I'll sing you to sleep.
Outside it is cold,
Field and wood are deep in snow,
But in thy little bed
It is nice and warm.

Sleep, my little doll,
Just go to sleep.
Close your eyes,
Sleep in peace.
Quickly the night is going,
Before we would have thought.

It's tomorrow already, eight in the morning,
And we are awake.
I wish you a good day,
I put on your dress.
Feed you a little porridge,
Eat it up with me.

And then we go to Grandmother's,
Haissassassa!
Then we go, you and I.
Hurray, how happy I am!
Good day, Grandmother.
Now we are there.

Hoffmann von Fallersleben
1778-1874

Big Doll and Little Doll

(Original German title: *Puppe und Püppchen*)

Big Doll: Little doll, you give yourself endless trouble.
You never learned to sit properly,
So try it, the way you see me do it.

Little Doll: I have done it already, but I think
I have no joints in my knees.

Then the child took them up
And said with a laugh:
"I will put the argument immediately to an end.
Both you dolls, small and large,
Are merely poor dumb things."
She threw them quickly
Into their chest,
Where they would be sure
To be quiet.

From *Fables for Children (Fabeln für Kinder)*, by Wilhelm Hey
1789-1854

Fable

(Original German title: *Fabel*)

Little doll, now look, I have taken the greatest
Pains with you.
I would like to make something clear to you:
I teach you the most beautiful things,
But you make no effort to learn.
You are so silly in the evening, and also in the morning.

The doll didn't cry about it.
The child didn't mean it to sound so bad.
She knew the doll couldn't do anything about it.
So she laid her down and left her in peace,
Went out and found herself a book
And learned from it many good things.

From *Fables for Children (Fabeln für Kinder)*, by Wilhelm Hey
1789-1854

French Dolls

Bisque, French, Jumeau, marked *Déposé E9J;* on the body *Jumeau Medaille d'Or Paris.*
Expressive doll on page 35 was made about 1879. She has swivel head with fixed, blue, glass eyes. Jointed body is composition. This doll is also pictured on page 15.

Bisque, French, Jumeau, marked *Déposé Tête Jumeau Bte S.G.D.G.v 12xx.*
This doll was made about 1890. She has a beautifully painted swivel head with fixed, blue paperweight eyes. Her body is composition.

Bisque, French, Jumeau, marked *Déposé Tête Jumeau 10 V;* on the body *Bébé Jumeau Bte. S. G. D. G. — Déposé.*
Jumeau is famous for his dolls' beautiful, expressive eyes. This doll has large, fixed, blue paperweight eyes.

Bisque, French, Jumeau, marked _Tête Jumeau 9;_ on the body _Jumeau Medaille d'Or Paris._ Made about 1890, this doll has original blond mohair wig. Swivel head has fixed, blue paperweight eyes and closed mouth. Jointed body is composition.

Bisque, French, Jumeau, marked _Déposé E 8 J;_ on the body _Jumeau Medaille d'Or Paris._ She has swivel head with expressive, fixed, blue paperweight eyes and closed mouth. Made about 1878, doll has jointed, composition body.

Bisque, French, Jumeau, marked *4;* on the body *Jumeau Medaille d'Or Paris.*
Swivel head on this doll has been carefully toned. She has large, fixed, blue eyes and closed mouth. Wood-and-composition body is ball-jointed.

Bisque, French, Jumeau, marked *E J 7;* on the body *Jumeau Medaille d'Or Paris.*
Made about 1878, this doll has swivel head with closed mouth and fixed, blue paperweight eyes. Jointed body with unjointed wrists is wood and composition.

This *Long-Face Jumeau* is described on facing page.

40

Bisque, French, Jumeau, marked *12*; on the body *Jumeau Medaille d'Or Paris.*

Jumeau Triste (Long-Face Jumeau or *Sad Jumeau)* is a rare doll made about 1878. She has swivel head of finest bisque, with fixed, blue paperweight eyes and closed mouth. Her name comes from her serious, thoughtful expression. Doll has original human-hair wig on cork pate. Ball-jointed body is wood and composition.

Bisque, French, Jumeau, marked *Déposé Tête Jumeau Bte. S.G.D.G. 10v;* on the body *Bébé Jumeau Bte. S.G.D.G. Déposé.*
This doll has swivel head with closed mouth and large, fixed, brown paperweight eyes. Made about 1895, she has ball-jointed, wood-and-composition body.

Bisque, marked *J.*
This doll has swivel head with fixed, brown paperweight eyes and closed mouth. Jointed body is composition.

42

Bisque, French, possibly Gaultier.
Polichinelle wears original costume with lace collar and lump in front and back—one symbolizing money, the other, luck. Body is stuffed with sawdust. Arms and legs are wood. Head is beautifully painted, with closed mouth and fixed, blue eyes.

Bisque, French, Gaultier, marked *F.G.*
Fixed, glass eyes of this doll have an unusual blue shade. Doll also has a heavily painted, closed mouth and jointed, composition body.

Bisque, French, head by Gaultier, body by Gesland, marked *F.8 G;* on the body *A. Gesland Fque. de Bébés & Têtes Incassables Bte. S.G.D.G.*
Doll at left, made about 1878, has swivel head with fixed, blue-gray paperweight eyes. Jointed body by A. Gesland, Paris, is wood and composition. On her left side is drawstring for voice box that says "Mama" and "Papa."

Bisque, French, Gaultier, marked *F.10 G.*
Premiere Gaultier, in center, has swivel head with closed mouth and fixed, blue-gray paperweight eyes. Ball-jointed body is wood and composition. Doll was made about 1878. She is also pictured on pages 4 and 8.

Bisque, French, possibly Gaultier.
Polichinelle, at right, is described on page 43.

44

**Bisque, French, head by
Gaultier, body by
Gesland, marked *F.8 G.;*
on the body *A. Gesland
Fque. de Bébés & Têtes
Incassables Bte. S.G.D.G.***
Doll at right is described
on page 44.

46

Bisque, French, head by Gaultier, body by Jumeau, marked _F G_ in a scroll above the number _9;_ on the body _Jumeau Medaille d'Or Paris._
Doll on left, made about 1880, has swivel head with closed mouth and fixed, brown paperweight eyes.

Bisque, French, Gaultier, marked _F. 7 G._
Doll on right has jointed, composition body and swivel head with brown, paperweight eyes. She was made about 1880.

Bisque, French, Gaultier, marked *F. 7 G.* Doll at right is described on page 47.

Bisque, French, head by Gaultier, body by Gesland, marked *F. 11 G.* Made about 1878, the doll on facing page has a beautiful swivel head with expressive, fixed, blue-gray paperweight eyes and closed mouth. Jointed body is metal with tricot covering. Hands and feet are wood.

Bisque, possibly French. This unsigned doll has a child's astonished expression. Swivel head has open mouth and fixed, blue paperweight eyes. Body has straight, movable legs and arms. When her arms are extended and she is pulled forward by her hands, an apparatus inside enables her to walk and move her head right and left.

Bisque, French, Steiner, marked *Fre A 13.*
Doll on left was made by Jules Nicholas Steiner, Paris, about 1890. She has finely tinted and painted swivel head, with closed mouth and fixed, blue paperweight eyes. Jointed wood body has typical spread fingers.

Bisque, French, Jumeau, marked *Tête Jumeau 9;* on the body *Jumeau Medaille d'Or Paris.*
Doll on right has swivel head with fixed, blue paperweight eyes, closed mouth and original blond mohair wig. She is also pictured on page 38.

Bisque, French, Gaultier, marked *F. 9 G.*
Premiere Gaultier, made about 1875, has delicately painted swivel head, closed mouth and fixed, brown paperweight eyes. Ball-jointed body is composition.

Bisque, French, Steiner, marked *ST. C. 2;* with signature *Bte. = S.g. D. g. J Bourgoin Sr* = handwritten in red ink.

Made about 1885, this beautiful doll has expressive face. Radiant, gray paperweight eyes can be opened and closed by lever behind left ear. She has a finely painted, closed mouth and jointed, composition body.

Bisque, French, Steiner, marked *Ste C 1.*
This doll was made about 1885. She has an intricately painted swivel head with closed mouth and fixed, blue paperweight eyes. Jointed body is composition and wood with wrist joints.

Bisque, French, Steiner, marked *Steiner Paris Fre. A 15;* on the body *Jumeau Medaille d'Or Paris 1889.*
This automatic Walking Doll was made about 1889. She has carefully painted swivel head with closed mouth and fixed, blue paperweight eyes. Jointed composition-and-wood body is well proportioned, with built-in walking mechanism. Windup key with locking lever is on right side.

Bisque, French, Schmitt, marked on neck and body with coat of arms that includes crossed hammers, and with *SCH.* Schmitt, Paris, made this doll about 1880. She has finely painted swivel head with closed mouth and fixed, blue-gray paperweight eyes. Her body of composition and wood has molded anatomical details.

Bisque, French, Steiner, marked *St. C. 2,* with signature *Bte.=S.g.D.g J Bourgoin Sr =* handwritten in red ink. Lever behind left ear controls opening and closing of gray paperweight eyes. Doll's jointed body is composition. She was made about 1885.

Bisque, French, Schmitt, marked on neck and body with coat of arms that includes crossed hammers, and with *SCH.* Doll has swivel head with closed mouth and fixed, bright-blue paperweight eyes. Ball-jointed body, made about 1878, is composition and wood.

Bisque, French, Schmitt.
This doll has swivel head
with bright-blue
paperweight eyes. Her
body is composition and
wood.

This doll has blue paperweight eyes and a full, closed mouth that is beautifully painted. Bisque forearms and hands have exquisite form. The doll's body, made about 1879, is kid. Shoulder plate has molded breast, as with most Bru dolls with kid bodies. Lower legs and feet are wood.

60

Bisque, French, Bru, marked *Bru Jne No 7* on the neck and shoulder plate.
This doll, shown in different costumes, was made about 1880. She has a swivel head with fixed, blue paperweight eyes and closed mouth. Body is kid. Arms and hands are bisque; lower legs and feet are wood. Shoulder plate has molded breast. Doll's wardrobe includes dresses, bonnets, purses, coat and fan.

Bisque, French, Bru, marked *Bru Jne. 8;* **on the shoulder plate** *Bru Jne 9.*
Doll at top and on opposite page has swivel head, expressive face, carefully painted, closed mouth and fixed, blue paperweight eyes. Body is kid, with wood arms and legs. Bisque shoulder plate has molded breast.

Bisque, French, Bru, marked *Bru Jne. No. 7* **on the neck and shoulder plate.**
Doll at bottom is described on page 63.

Detail of larger doll
described on opposite
page, dressed here in
different costume.

**Bisque, French, Bru,
marked** *Bru Jne 9;* **on the
back** *Bru Jne 6 N;* **on the
shoe** *Bru Jeune Paris;* **on
label on the body** *Bébé
Bru Bte. S.G.D.G.*
An expressive face
characterizes this doll,
made about 1875. She
has a smoothly molded
swivel head, closed mouth
and fixed, dark,
paperweight eyes.
Shoulder plate has
molded breast. Body is
painstakingly worked kid.
Lower legs and feet are
wood. Forearms and
hands are bisque.

**Bisque, French, Bru,
marked *Bru Jne 14*.**
This Bru doll has a
beautifully molded swivel
head, composition body
and voice box that says
"Mama." The expressive
head has closed mouth
and large, fixed, blue-gray
paperweight eyes.
Composition body is
joined in the middle,
where the voice box has
been inserted. The body
is held together by a
leather band. Pull-cord on
side of body controls
voice mechanism. Doll is
also pictured in different
dress on page 19.

Bisque, French, Bru, marked *Bru Jne 5* on the neck and shoulder plate; on label on the body *Bébé Bru Bte. S.G.D.G.*
This exceptionally lovely doll is in perfect condition. She has a finely molded swivel head and expressive features, including a closed mouth with full lips and fixed, bright-blue paperweight eyes. Doll has typical Bru body of finely worked kid, carefully molded bisque forearms, and wood lower legs and feet. Shoulder plate has molded breast.

Bisque, French, Bru, marked *Bru Jne 13* on the neck and shoulder plate. This Bru doll, shown in different costumes, has an unusual, finely drawn face. She has an accentuated upper lip, closed mouth and large, blue paperweight eyes. Her swivel head, made about 1880, is finest quality bisque. Shoulder plate with molded breast is carefully worked. Molded arms and hands have naturalistic elbows. Body is kid. Legs and feet are wood. From Jackie Jacobs Collection, London.

Bisque, French, Bru, marked with circle and dot with crescent; on the forehead S.G.D.G; on the shoulder plate 8.
This doll has a distinctive molded head like that of *Bébé Teteur* on page 74, but with a more mature facial expression. Mouth is open-closed with faintly indicated, painted upper teeth. She has large, almond-shaped, brown paperweight eyes. Swivel head, shoulder plate with molded breast, arms and hands are fine bisque. Body is kid.

Bisque, French, Bru, marked *Bru Jne 11* on the neck and shoulder plate.
Closed mouth and large, paperweight eyes are typical of the expressive faces made by Bru. The swivel head, shoulder plate with molded breast and beautifully shaped arms and hands are fine bisque. Body is kid. Lower legs and feet are wood. From Jackie Jacobs Collection, London.

Bisque, French, Bru, marked with circle and dot.
The beautifully molded head is typical of the series represented by this doll. Mouth is open-closed with prominent lower lip. Doll has large, fixed, brown paperweight eyes. Forearms and hands are bisque. Body is dark kid. Shoulder plate has molded breast.

Bisque, French, Bru, marked *Bru Jne 5 T;* on the shoulder plate *1 T.*
Bébé Teteur (Nursing Baby) was patented in 1879. Swivel head and shoulder plate with molded breast are bisque. The doll has large, fixed, brown paperweight eyes and an open mouth. Body is kid. Forearms and hands are carefully shaped bisque. Doll can drink from a bottle. A key is located in the neck. When turned to the right, the key activates suction in rubber reservoir behind doll's mouth. Suction empties doll's bottle into reservoir.

All-bisque, possibly German.
Large doll at left is described below. Small doll at right was made about 1900.

Bisque, French, Bru, marked *Bru Jne 3;* **on the left shoulder** *Bru;* **on the right shoulder** *No 2 T;* **on label on the shoulder plate** *Bébé Bru Bte. S.G.D.G.*
Made about 1880, this doll has a swivel head with closed mouth and fixed, brown paperweight eyes. Shoulder plate has molded breast. Body is kid. Arms, hands and legs are wood. Also shown on page 103.

**Bisque, French, Petit &
Dumontier, marked *P 5 D.***
This rare doll, by Petit &
Dumontier, Paris, was
made about 1885. She
has a swivel head with
closed mouth and large,
fixed, blue paperweight
eyes. Her ball-jointed,
composition body is made
of 19 pieces. Hands are
metal.

**Bisque, French, May
Brothers, marked
Mascotte J; on the body
*Bébé Mascotte Paris.***
Doll by May Brothers Co.,
Paris, has bisque swivel
head with expressive
facial features, including
closed mouth and large,
fixed, brown paperweight
eyes. Body is wood.

Bisque, marked *131*.
Belton-Type Doll has a finely painted swivel head with closed mouth and fixed, blue, glass eyes. Jointed body is composition.

Bisque, marked *120 9*, and with a cross.
Belton-Type Doll has a fair complexion and a swivel head with closed mouth and bright-blue eyes. Eyelashes and brows are especially well-painted. Jointed body is composition.

Bisque.
Polichinelle on bird of paradise is unsigned, but head is possibly Gaultier. Doll has closed mouth and fixed, blue paperweight eyes. This photo shows the original costume. Bird of paradise is brightly painted papier-mâché. It stands on a green base with four wheels, which move. When bird rolls forward, *Polichinelle* raises right arm and moves head right and left. Two small clowns, by A. Lanternier & Co., Limoges, France, have swivel heads and movable but unjointed arms and legs.

Bisque, possibly French. Clowns have brightly painted papier-mâché heads and movable blue eyes. They wear original costumes.

Bisque, possibly French.
Fashion-Type Doll has swivel head with fixed, blue, glass eyes and closed mouth. Body is leather.

Bisque, French, head possibly by Gaultier, body by Roullet & Decamps.
Walking Doll by Roullet & Decamps, Paris, was made about 1880. She wears original clothing. Doll has blue eyes and closed mouth. Roullet & Decamps were famous for mechanical dolls, which won numerous medals at Parisian exhibitions.

Bisque, French, possibly Gaultier.
Fashion-Type Doll is beautifully clothed in original apparel, including purse and parasol. She has beautiful swivel head on shoulder plate. Jointed wood body has double joints in upper arms, elbows and legs. Doll was made about 1870.

**Bisque, possibly French,
head possibly by
Gaultier, body possibly
by Roullet & Decamps.**
Walking Doll has fixed,
blue paperweight eyes
and closed mouth.

Bisque, possibly French.
Fashion-Type Doll has
fine swivel head. Fixed,
blue paperweight eyes
and closed mouth
contribute to lovely facial
expression. Body is
leather.

Bisque, French, Huret.
Fashion-Type Doll was made by Huret, Paris, about 1861. This doll has an exquisitely formed swivel head on bisque shoulder plate. Plate was patented by Huret in 1861. Face is beautifully painted. Eyes, whose lids may be molded, convey gentle expression. Mouth is closed. Body is leather, with bisque forearms. Smaller doll on right, opposite page, possibly by Huret. Both dolls wear original clothes. From Jackie Jacobs Collection, London.

Bisque, possibly French.
This Fashion-Type Doll has bright bisque forearms and hands, and wears original dress. She is from Jackie Jacobs Collection, London.

Bisque, possibly French.
Beautiful original dress with muff adorns Fashion-Type Doll. She has swivel head with fixed, dark-blue, glass eyes. Body is leather. Jointed legs are wood. Arms and hands are bisque. From Jackie Jacobs Collection, London.

Bisque, French, Bru.
Unsigned Fashion-Type Doll has fixed, glass eyes and closed mouth. Body is leather with ball-jointed, wood arms. She wears original clothes.

Bisque.
Leather body of this Fashion-Type Doll has movable hips. She has a swivel head with fixed, dark, glass eyes and closed mouth. Forearms and hands are bisque. She wears original costume.

Bisque, possibly French, possibly Gaultier.
Height is distinguishing characteristic of this Fashion-Type Doll. She is more than 3 feet tall. Made about 1870, this doll has an exquisite head of almost-white bisque, with delicate painting and tinting. She has a closed mouth and fixed, blue paperweight eyes. Head rests on bisque shoulder plate attached to kid body. She is clothed in beautiful damask dress, rich with trim and lace. German Character Doll marked *126* by Simon & Halbig sits in stroller. She has bisque swivel head with glass, blue sleep eyes and open mouth. Composition body has unjointed arms and legs.

Bisque, French, Petit & Dumontier, marked *P 4D*.
Doll by Petit & Dumontier, Paris, has swivel head with closed mouth and fixed, brown paperweight eyes. Wig is sheepskin. Ball-jointed body is composition with metal hands. Doll was made about 1880 and has original clothes. From Jackie Jacobs Collection, London.

Bisque, French, possibly Jumeau.
This doll has an unmarked swivel head with closed mouth and fixed, almond-shaped, glass eyes. Jointed body is composition and wood. Doll wears lovely, original clothes. From Jackie Jacobs Collection, London.

Bisque, French, possibly Jumeau.
A grown-up expression characterizes this doll. She has large, fixed, brown paperweight eyes and a closed mouth. Molded swivel head rests on ball-jointed composition-and-wood body. From Jackie Jacobs Collection, London.

Bisque, French, possibly Steiner.
This unusual doll has prominent, oversize, blue, glass eyes, with fiber irises and large pupils. Jointed body is composition and wood. Doll wears decorative original costume. From Jackie Jacobs Collection, London.

Bisque, French, possibly Huret.
Rare Character Doll has expressive swivel head with delicately painted blue eyes and closed mouth. Jointed body is composition. From Jackie Jacobs Collection, London.

Bisque, French, Thuillier, marked *A 11 T.*
Rare doll from A. Thuillier, Paris, made about 1880, is shown here and on page 95. Doll has well-proportioned swivel head with fixed, almond-shaped, blue paperweight eyes. Closed mouth has hint of smile. Jointed body is composition and wood. She wears original clothes.

From a Child to a Doll

(Original German title: *Einem Kind zu einer Puppe*)

Rock, child, that wonderful being
That you have in your arms!
She almost seems without life
With her stuck-on hair.
On her cheeks the two garish red spots
Are quite bold.
Only the dress with its white bow
Is like yours, bright and green.

There are important things to do:
Give her a little baby food,
Touch her gently with sweet kisses.
She will eat, she will sleep.
Many times, naturally, she sleeps quite naked,
And she may eat the plate clean.
Think of her! She is still small,
And you yourself are already big.

Behold, she promises more!
Just lay her down and sit her up;
See how nicely she can open
And close her eyelids.
Every game that you play
Teaches her and instructs her
As you have been instructed,
Until she lives within your soul,
Until she laughs and cries like you.
As you rock her in your arms,
You become, in just a moment,
Before you know it,
A grown-up, smiling, serious mother.
She closes her eyes as you close yours:
Two sweet precious stones
Of inexhaustible deepest blue.

Max Kommerell
1902-1944

Bisque, French, marked *H*.
Blue paperweight eyes
are slightly different sizes,
giving this rare doll an
unusual appearance.
Jointed body is
composition. Swivel head
is well-shaped, with
carefully painted features.

The Doll

(Original German title: *Die Puppe*)

My little dress is fiery red,
My face still bears a festive light,
Like the mast of a sailboat.

I would bestow on that dear child
Who so gently talks to me
A kiss as her mother taught,
And would help her say her evening prayer.

She spoke beside my ear and cheek,
Gestured with her hand.
Silent words I spoke to her,
Which she understood well.

When she tosses a kerchief on my little carriage
And gives it a quick shove,
Her smile would be to me
As a finch flying in a dream.

I have known misery.
Often on days when she was sick,
Hungry and forlorn,
I lay there on the stairs.

Then the cheek rejected me
That had been pressed warm against me,
Leaving me to the grass and darkness,
That soaked me with the dew.

Far from that June morning dew
And from that fair-skinned child,
My gray-fleeced mother
Lifts me trembling from the closet.

My dirty eyes look out at her
From beneath blond hair
Stained by play and grass,
And by her fifth year.

Gertrud Kolmar
1894-1943

The Toy Dog
and Dolls

Bisque, French, Bru, marked *Bru Jne 3;* on the left shoulder *Bru;* on the right shoulder *No 2 T;* on label on the shoulder plate *Bébé Bru Bte. S.G.D.G.*
The doll shown on page 103 has swivel head on bisque shoulder plate. Body is kid. Doll was made about 1880. She is also pictured on page 76.

Bisque, French, Schmitt.
Doll on right, facing page, is also shown below. Doll on left has similar features. Walking poodle dates from about 1900.

Bisque, French, Schmitt. This doll, made about 1878, has an especially fine swivel head with closed mouth and fixed, bright-blue paperweight eyes. Ball-jointed body is composition and wood. Doll is also pictured on page 59.

Bisque, French.
Mignonnettes (Little Darlings) from Paris, made about 1880, have bisque hands. Dolls wear original clothes.

Bisque, French, Bru, marked with circle and dot; on the body *Bébé Brevete S.G.D.G.*
This doll can be fed. Liquid goes into a rubber ball inside the head. When doll is full, pressure on the head forces liquid through the body to the shoes, then out through a valve. This doll's head, lower arms, hands, lower legs and feet are highest quality bisque.

**Bisque, German, head by
Simon & Halbig, body by
Kämmer & Reinhardt,
marked** *Simon & Halbig
K (star) R.*
This doll has a swivel
head with open mouth and
carefully painted
eyebrows. Glass, blue
sleep eyes have real
eyelashes. Ball-jointed
body is composition and
wood.

Bisque, possibly French.
Clowns in original
costumes have brightly
painted papier-mâché
heads and movable blue
eyes. Dolls are also
pictured on page 79.

Mignonnettes
and Fashion-Type Dolls

Both dolls on page 109
have original clothes.

**All-bisque, possibly
French.**
Blond mohair wig
distinguishes doll at left.
She has fixed, blue, glass
eyes.

**All-bisque, possibly
French.**
Doll at right has fixed,
brown, glass eyes and a
closed mouth. Small
all-bisque dolls can be
used in dollhouses.

All-bisque.
These dolls have molded and painted shoes. Facial features include fixed, glass eyes and closed mouths. Doll on left wears original clothes.

All-bisque, possibly German.
This doll has blue, glass eyes and a closed mouth. Shoes are painted.

All-bisque.
Some of these dolls, made about 1880, wear decorative, original clothes. They have buckled shoes and stockings. Boy doll is on stagecoach. He has fixed, brown, glass eyes and a closed mouth. His wig is mohair.

Bisque.
The face on this doll is carefully painted, with open mouth and fixed, brown eyes. Doll wears original velvet suit. He has molded and painted shoes and stockings.

Bisque.
Shoes and stockings are painted on this doll. She has fixed, blue, glass eyes and closed mouth.

All-bisque.
This doll has painted shoes and stockings. Facial features include fixed, brown, glass eyes and closed mouth.

Bisque, possibly German.
Dollhouse Doll has a
shoulder plate with
molded breast. Body is
white fabric. Arms and
lower legs are bisque,
with molded and painted
shoes and stockings.

The Toy Store

(Original German title: *Spielzeugladen*)

There goes the train on a shining track,
Through tunnel and town in circles, in circles.
And there go autos being driven and turned,
And dredges and cranes being cranked and swiveled,
And airplanes and ships with rudder and sail,
And children's blocks, games, and books and nine-pins,
And rollers and sleighs, and a zoo with giraffes,
And lions and bears and jolly monkeys—
Oh, my—
Behind the panes, behind the glass!

There goes the train on a shining track,
Through tunnel and town in circles, in circles.
And there go autos being driven and turned,
And dredges and cranes being cranked and swiveled,
And airplanes and ships with rudder and sail,
And children's blocks, games, books and nine-pins,
And rollers and sleighs, and a zoo with giraffes,
And lions and bears and jolly monkeys—
Oh, my—
Behind the panes, behind the glass!

Ursula Wölfel

My Childhood Years

(Original German title: *Meine Kinderjahre*)

We could almost count on our fingers the days until Christmas, when something happened that put us in a terrible state: Our dolls disappeared!

We felt all was lost. A complete doll emigration had occurred. The bed in which just yesterday Fritzi had laid her eldest daughter, Big Christine, was empty. Christine's family had fled! It was as if they had never lived here.

My blond Fanchette, named for the color of her hair, was not to be found. We rummaged in vain in our drawers, searched in all the cupboards and corners. We ran into the nursery and accused our poor little brother of the theft.

We didn't remember that in previous years we had experienced the same grief shortly before Christmas, only to find our dolls under the tree on Christmas morning. They looked so beautiful with their flowing locks and shining porcelain faces!

Oh, we were such dumb children! I don't believe any children today are quite as dumb.

Marie von Ebner-Eschenbach
1830-1916

Dolls at Christmas

Bisque, French, Bru, marked *Bru Jne No 7* on the neck and shoulder plate.
Extensive wardrobe accompanying doll on page 119 includes bonnets, dresses, purses and fan. She has shoulder plate with molded breast. Arms and hands are bisque, lower legs and feet are wood. Doll also shown on pages 62 and 63.

Bisque, possibly French.
Doll on opposite page has composition body.

Bisque, possibly French.
At left is toy horse and Fashion-Type Doll.

Bisque, German, König & Wernicke, marked *K & W 1070.*
The Character Doll above by König & Wernicke, Waltershausen, Germany, has a swivel head with lashed, glass, brown sleep eyes. Ball-jointed body is composition and wood. She was made about 1912.

Bisque, German, Kestner, marked *152.*
Made about 1885, the doll above has a swivel head with glass, brown sleep eyes and a closed mouth. Ball-jointed body is composition and wood. She was made by Kestner, Waltershausen, Germany.

Bisque, French, Bru, marked with circle and dot; on the body *Bébé Brevete S.G.D.G.*
The doll at right has fixed, blue paperweight eyes. She is also pictured on page 107.

Bisque, French, Jumeau, marked *Déposé Tête Jumeau 10 V;* on the body *Bébé Jumeau Bte. S.G.D.G.—Déposé.* Doll at right has fixed, blue paperweight eyes and jointed, composition body. Also shown on page 36.

Bisque, French. Doll on opposite page, left, marked *F 7G,* was made about 1880 by Gaultier. Doll on right, also by Gaultier, is marked *F 6G.* She was made about 1885. Doll on chair is all-bisque.

Bisque, German, Simon & Halbig, marked *S & H 12.* The doll above has a swivel head with large, glass, blue sleep eyes. Ball-jointed body is composition.

Bisque, German, head by Simon & Halbig, body by Kämmer & Reinhardt, marked *S & H K(star)R 34* The doll at right has a swivel head and small, glass, blue sleep eyes. Also pictured on page 28.

Bisque, French, Jumeau, marked *Tête Jumeau v 10;* on the body *Jumeau Medaille d'Or Paris.* The doll above has a swivel head with open mouth and fixed, brown paperweight eyes. Jointed body is composition.

Bisque, German, head by Simon & Halbig, body by Kämmer & Reinhardt, marked K (star) R 117/A. *Mein Liebling,* at right, has swivel head with closed, pouty mouth and small, fixed, brown, glass eyes. Ball-jointed body is composition and wood.

Bisque, French. Boy Character Doll on opposite page, left, was made by Société Française de Fabrication de Bébés & Jouets, Paris. He is marked *S.F.B.J. 236 Paris.* He has a finely tinted swivel head with happy child's face, small, brown, glass sleep eyes, and an open-closed mouth with two molded upper teeth. Body is composition, with movable, unjointed arms and legs. Largest doll on right is Belton-Type Doll marked *131.* She has a closed head with two small holes in the crown. She is strung with rubber cord inserted through holes. She has a swivel head with closed mouth and fixed, bright-blue eyes. Jointed body is composition.

Bisque, possibly French. The doll at right has a delicately painted swivel head with fixed, blue paperweight eyes. Mouth is closed. Jointed body is composition.

Bisque, French, Bru, marked Bru Jne R 10. Doll at left has a swivel head with closed mouth and fixed, brown paperweight eyes. Jointed body is composition and wood.

Play

(Original German title: *Spielen*)

Play is a dream, a fantasy, a way to lose oneself. It is a creative event that originates in the subconscious and unfolds freely. Play is not restricted by age. The blissful state a child sinks into can be experienced by grown-ups. It can be very soothing to adults who have kept a little of the child within themselves.

Any work done wholeheartedly may be a form of play. Certainly this is the case in creative professions. Painters get great pleasure from looking at their pictures. Dancers experience deep contentment when they execute proper moves. Workers and gardeners feel the same when they successfully complete a task. Children have similar experiences when they build a tower of blocks, or a sand castle, or follow a dragon with their eyes.

Play is full of surprises, unexpected joy and disappointment. But even the setbacks kindle the imagination, inspiring people to pick up the thread again and spin it out to the end. The secret of play is that it awakens unknown skills that give people great joy and the feeling of having created something. It is constant advancement, but is not perceived as such.

Ursula Brecht